GOD
IS MY
PROVIDER

IN YOUR DAILY JOURNEY THROUGH GOD'S WORD, USE THIS BOOKMARK AS A REMINDER THAT GOD PROVIDES.

TEAR ALONG PERFORATION

CROWN FINANCIAL MINISTRIES™

GOD PROVIDES™ LEARNING EXPERIENCE

WIDOW AND OIL
WHAT DO YOU HAVE?
2 Kings 4:1-7

JEREMIAH'S CALL
GODS' DESIGN FOR HOPE
Jeremiah 29:1-14

ABRAM'S REWARD
MAKING MAJOR LIFE CHOICES
Genesis 12-15:6

ABRAHAM AND ISAAC
MINE OR HIS?
Genesis 22:1-18

RICH MAN AND LAZARUS
MY HEART DECISIONS AFFECT ETERNITY
Luke 16:19-31

LIFTED UP
MY HOPE FOR THE FUTURE
John 3:1-17

CROWN.ORG/GODPROVIDES
1-800-249-6320

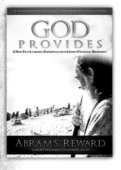

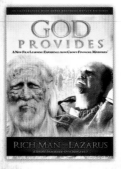
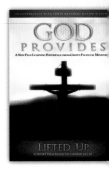

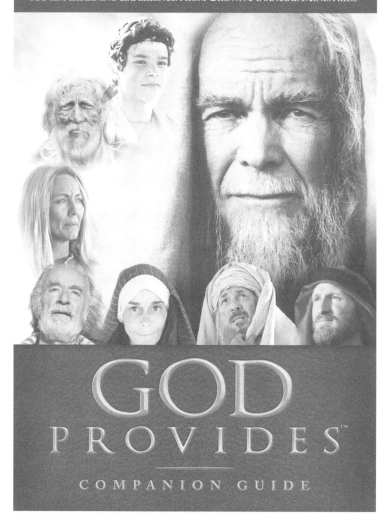

GOD PROVIDES™

COMPANION GUIDE

CROWN FINANCIAL MINISTRIES™
Crown.org/GodProvides

This Companion Guide is intended for use with the *God Provides*™ *Learning Experience*. The films have not yet been rated. We recommend previewing the films to determine if they are appropriate for younger viewers.

ISBN: 978-1-56427-266-9

GOD PROVIDES™ is a trademark of Crown Financial Ministries, Inc.

In Canada, go to CrownCanada.ca or call 1-866-401-0626.

Scriptures designated (NIV) taken from the Holy Bible, New International Version® NIV®.
Copyright © 1973, 1978, 1984 by International Bible Society. Used by permission. All rights reserved worldwide.

Scriptures designated (NASB) taken from the New American Standard Bible®, Copyright © 1960,1962,1963,1968,1971, 1972,1973,1975,1977,1995 by The Lockman Foundation. Used by permission.

July 2009 Printing

Contents

This Companion Guide is designed primarily for use by small groups and for individual study. In addition to the transition cues provided in the main session pages, the Facilitator's Guide supplies helpful tips for opening and closing a session, keeping discussions on track, personal and group activities, and other supporting information. Additional Companion Guides sold separately.

If you have purchased a single film from this series, please use the Learning Experience Session in this book corresponding with that film.

The Family Guide has been added to help parents convey the key concepts from each session in simplified terms.

Be sure to register at Crown.org/GodProvides for free access to downloadable worksheets, articles, tips, and links.

Introduction

Welcome! I'm both excited and humbled that you've decided to join us in this *God Provides*™ *Learning Experience*.

I'm excited because we're engaging in a process of discovering new aspects of God's awesome love and faithfulness. As a result, we'll increase our trust in Him to provide for our deepest needs.

And I'm humbled to have been entrusted with sharing these accounts from the Bible—God's Word—through the special medium of film. We've taken care to present the biblical accounts in these dramatic film adaptations as accurately as possible. Although not the written Word, these stories contain biblical truths that will lead to life-change.

This Companion Guide is no ordinary workbook. Each section is designed to be part of a true "learning experience," carefully crafted to guide, support, and even challenge us along the way. Lasting impact comes when we engage all of these key areas:

 Our Head – as we view and discuss the films

 Our Heart – as we reflect on the personal implications of these stories

 Our Hands – as we apply our discoveries through meaningful activities

My prayer is that you will be deeply impacted by taking this journey and will share it with those whom you love. Plans are now underway to translate and distribute these films worldwide. People from every economic and social background from around the globe—rich and poor, readers and nonreaders—will be joining us on this *God Provides*™ journey. All will be able to view these films and benefit from the compelling financial and life lessons they present. You can join in this mission and keep track of our progress at Crown.org/GodProvides.

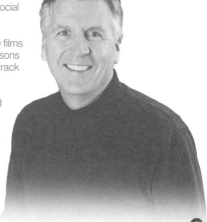

Finally, remember that God is our ultimate guide and teacher on this journey. My prayer for you is that His Holy Spirit will bless you with life's true reward—the infinite riches of knowing, loving, and serving Jesus Christ.

Chuck Bentley

Chuck Bentley
CEO, Crown Financial Ministries

Acknowledgments

I am grateful to Sharon Epps and her incredible team—John Smith, Amanda Johnson, Josh Merriam, Mark Nunnally, Kevin Light, Jason Gazaway, Robin Greene, Michael McNeilly, Jim Armstrong, Chuck Thompson, Jim Henry, Scott Grant, Hope Welborn, and Sean Allen—for their work on the new learning system. With valuable input from many others, this team wrote and assembled the learning experience around each film. (They would like your feedback and testimonies at Crown.org/GodProvides.)

And my thanks also go to Stephen Sorenson for his writing assistance and developmental input for this Companion Guide.

Chuck Bentley

WIDOW and OIL

"What Do You Have?"

Adapted from 2 Kings 4:1-7

Warm Up: *Participate in the short exercise given in the Facilitator's Guide on page 42.*

Overview

This section puts the film into context, setting the stage for discussion after you view the film.

We all experience difficult and often painful circumstances as a result of our actions, other people's actions, or things beyond our control. Major life issues—such as the death of a loved one, loss of employment, serious illness, financial pressures—can be overwhelming.

The God of the Bible, whose ways are far beyond what we can think or imagine, invites us to humble ourselves and turn to Him for help. When we do, He provides answers to our deepest needs. Although God cares about our immediate needs, He is even more concerned about our relationship with Him. He desires for each of us to put our faith and trust in Him and be attentive to His direction.

During this session, we'll learn about a woman who faced an agonizing dilemma. She had meager resources, a seemingly impossible situation and no good solutions. But she did the only thing she could think to do—and her obedient faith and willingness to follow godly counsel led to incredible blessing from God.

Read *this film's foundational verses: 2 Kings 4:1-7*

Cue DVD: Feature Film - (12 minutes)

Discuss

These thought-provoking questions will help you discover the truths presented in the story. Study them on your own or discuss with others immediately after watching the film.

1 Imagine that you are in the widow's situation right now. The creditor has just told you the bad news, and you are paralyzed with fear. What might you do? Why?

2 How aware do you think the widow was of the God Elisha (and her late husband) served?

When did she first demonstrate faith?

What did she admit to Elisha right away?

3 If you were the widow, how might you have responded when Elisha wanted to know what she had in her little home?

How much value did she place on what she had?

4 Why do you think God chose to have the widow participate in her own provision? Why was it important for her children and neighbors to play a part as well?

Crying Out to God

Second Kings 4:1 reveals that the widow "cried out to Elisha," the prophet of God. And God, through Elisha, responded to her desperate need. God always responds when His people cry out to Him for help. Look up these Bible passages: Deuteronomy 26:6-9; Judges 15:18-19; 1 Kings 17:19-22; 2 Chronicles 32:20-23; Mark 10:46-52; Luke 17:11-14.

Reflect | *Take just a few minutes now to quietly reflect on these inward-directed questions.*

1 How has God provided for your needs, and how have you responded to Him?

2 In what way(s) might the steps the widow took to actively participate in resolving her situation relate to you and situations you face?

3 In which area(s) might you need to admit your need for help, place your faith and trust in God, and seek—and follow—godly, Bible-based counsel?

What may be keeping you from doing this?

God Can Use the Most Basic Things

It's easy to conclude that we don't already have what God might use to meet our needs. Jesus' disciples felt like this, too. Read Luke 9:12-17.

Sometimes God provides miraculously. Other times, we need to ask for help and "borrow jars," in effect, from other people. God often meets needs through the church—the body of people who follow Jesus. Yet some people find it difficult to ask for help.

 Cue DVD: Journey Notes - (2 minutes)

 **Journey Notes*** | *Chuck Bentley encourages you on your journey in this short "wrap up" presentation. Space is provided for you to jot down a few notes.*

an alternative, you
use the monologue
ey Character's
pective" (found in
tional Teaching on
VD).

Up Close

Chuck Bentley, executive producer of *God Provides*,™ says that the spark for the film series came while he was on a trip to Africa. There he saw the tremendous need for a way to teach essential Bible truths to non-readers.

Engage

We are able to engage most fully with the new insights we discover when we apply them in very practical ways.

Personal Activity

Perhaps you are facing a difficult situation, and you struggle to believe that God can work things out. If so, what small—or large—step can you take toward trusting God, and His perfect, sovereign will?

What Do You Have?

Write down what you have—however small—that God might use to help you through current or future hard times. (Possessions, skills, talents, etc.)

Activity Tip

Obtain a simple notebook in which you can record your thoughts, responses, struggles and prayers in your faith journey with God.

Possessions	Skills/Talents	People Who Can Help

You can download the "What Do You Have? Inventory" to help you organize this information. Visit *Crown.org/GodProvides* and follow the *Widow and Oil* links.

Group Activity

Take a quick assessment of your group and record the answers to the following questions:

1 **What Do You Have?** Make a list of the skills, talents, and resources available within your group. For instance, you may find some in your group who are skilled at home or auto repairs, or have surplus items, or are available for babysitting. (The "What Do You Have?" Inventory has a section for groups to record this information.)

2 **Who Can You Help?** Have the group brainstorm and identify an individual (or family) who faces a difficult situation. Then explore how your group might "partner" in offering help to them in the coming weeks. *(This exercise is to assess needs and get ideas from the group only. There will be a future group activity to perform the actual work your group chooses to do.)*

For Additional Exploration

Register online at Crown.org/GodProvides and follow the *Widow and Oil* links for more activities, **Next Step Resources**, and supporting materials such as • **Financial Stewardship Assessment** • **What Do You Have? Inventory**

JEREMIAH'S CALL

"God's Design for Hope"

Adapted from Jeremiah 29:1-14

 Warm Up: *Participate in the short exercise given in the Facilitator's Guide.*

Overview

This section puts the film into context, setting the stage for discussion after you view the film.

More than 2,500 years ago, exiled Jews from Judah were eking out an existence in Babylon. No doubt some remembered how King Nebuchadnezzar had besieged Jerusalem in 605 B.C. and carried some of Judah's gifted young men into exile. Later, more Babylonian troops transported additional Jews from Judah to Babylon and destroyed Jerusalem.

God caused these events because He loved His people too much to abandon them to their sinful ways. He used their hardships to discipline and teach them to obey Him. Only then, He knew, could they find true hope and purposeful living.

In Babylon, false Jewish prophets prophesied *"false visions, divinations, idolatries and the delusions of their own minds"* (Jeremiah 14:14 NIV) and evidently told the exiles not to serve the king of Babylon and his people.

God, however, had other plans. As illustrated in this session's film, through the prophet Jeremiah God spoke encouraging and unusual words that required the exiles to exercise great faith in God and do something unprecedented for exiles at that time in history to do.

 Read *this film's foundational verses:* Jeremiah 29:1-14.

 Cue DVD: Feature Film - (14 minutes)

Discuss | *These thought-provoking questions will help you discover the truths presented in the story. Study them on your own or discuss with others immediately after watching the film.*

1 What lessons did you learn from this film?

Verses to Ponder

"'For I know the plans I have for you, declares the Lord, 'plans to prosper you and not to harm you, plans to give you hope and a future. Then yo will call upon me and come and pray to me, and I will listen to you. You wi seek me and find me when you seek me with all your heart'" (Jeremiah 29:11-13 NIV).

2 Prior to the arrival of Jeremiah's message, the exiles must have been tempted to think that life would never return to "normal." How might their feelings compare with those of people who face difficult situations today?

3 Read Jeremiah 29:11-13 aloud (see the shaded box). What is significant about the phrase, "I know . . ."?

During difficult times, can we always recognize God's ongoing work in our lives and the world around us? Explain your answers.

In these verses, what did God ask the exiles to do in order to realize His gift of hope and a future?

What does this prophecy of Jeremiah reveal about the heart of God?

4 God told His people to settle where they were, build houses, marry, and plant gardens. He didn't rescue them from their problems immediately. What can we learn from this?

5 Imagine being the exiles who experienced the Babylonians' savagery. Now God has commanded them to put down roots in Babylon, seek its peace and prosperity, and even pray for it! What emotions do you think surfaced when they understood God's command? Why?

How can this apply to us in today's society?

Reflect

Take just a few minutes now to quietly reflect on these inward-directed questions.

1 How does a person "seek God with all of his or her heart"? (See Jeremiah 29:13.) Are you doing this? Read these verses before answering: Proverbs 3:5; 4:23-27; Joshua 22:5; Matthew 22:34-37; and Colossians 3:23.

2 Do you believe that God hears your prayers, cares about your situation, and wants you to pray for your governmental leaders? What is He teaching you these days about listening to His voice?

3 When you feel trapped in difficult circumstances and are losing hope, how might you benefit from remembering God's promise to give the Jewish exiles hope and a future?

Cue DVD: Journey Notes - (2 minutes)

Journey Notes*

Chuck Bentley encourages you on your journey in this short "wrap up" presentation. Space is provided for you to jot down a few notes.

n alternative, you
use the monologue
ey Character's
ective" (found in
ional Teaching on
VD).

How to Avoid Bad Counsel

Today some people speak falsely, seeking to influence our hearts and minds. See what these verses reveal about how we can detect and overcome lies: Hebrews 4:12; Psalm 24:4-5; James 1:15; and 1 John 4:1-3.

Engage

We are able to engage most fully with the new insights we discover when we apply them in very practical ways.

Personal Activity

Focus on cultivating a deeper relationship with God. He loves you and desires to unfold His plans for your life and give you renewed hope and purpose. Spend time with Him, through prayer and Bible study, and learn more about loving (obeying) Him. Within the next few days, take a Prayer Walk on your own, praying for local and national governmental leaders.

Which person(s) in your community might God want you to build a "no-strings-attached" relationship with—and prayerfully help to prosper? Pray about this, then take action.

Group Activity

Arrange for your group to take a Prayer Walk around your community. Start at the town hall or key governmental building. As you walk around various areas of your town or city, pray for God's blessing, the wisdom and prosperity of your leaders, and spiritual revival. Then sit down in a coffee shop or other location to talk about this special time and how you can continue to practice the discipline of prayer.

Prayer is Importan

If your group cannot do a Prayer Walk, set aside special prayer time within your group meeting.

For Additional Exploration

Register online at Crown.org/GodProvides and follow the *Jeremiah's Call* links for more activities, **Next Step Resources**, and supporting materials such as **Debt Reduction Plan • Job Satisfaction Survey • Free** *Personality I.D.*® **Profile**

ABRAM'S REWARD

"Making Major Life Choices"

Adapted from Genesis 12-15:6

Warm Up: *Participate in the short exercise given in the Facilitator's Guide.*

 Overview | *This section puts the film into context, setting the stage for discussion after you view the film.*

Under God's command, Abram left his home and journeyed to a new land, Canaan, with all his goods, his family, and his nephew Lot. The contrasts between the wise choices of Abram and the foolish choices of Lot provide valuable lessons for us today—contentment with less versus wanting more; loving people versus loving things; and giving versus taking.

Abram illustrated a loving attitude through his care for his nephew Lot, a willingness to take less by allowing Lot to make first choice when dividing the land, and a generous spirit by giving a tenth of the goods he collects in battle to Melchizedek, "priest of God Most High" (Genesis 14:18).

Lot's superficial decision to choose the beautiful land near Sodom becomes his undoing. Yet Abram displays great trust in God, pursuing the armies of the invading kings with relatively few men in order to rescue Lot.

Like Abram, are you generous? Do you trust God, or is fear preventing you from releasing control of your life to Him? Are you willing to seek the counsel necessary in order to make wise decisions? Let the examples you see in this film encourage you to bring your giving, trust, and decision-making into line with the principles of God's Word.

 Read *this selection of key verses:* Genesis 13:11-13; 14:14-20; 15:1-5.

 Cue DVD: Feature Film - (16 minutes)

🗣 Discuss

These thought-provoking questions will help you discover the truths presented in the story. Study them on your own or discuss with others immediately after watching the film.

① How was Abram's trust in God, love for people, and generosity demonstrated . . .

In his choice to leave his home country?

During his discussion with Lot about where to live?

In his response to learning about Lot's capture?

In his dealings with Melchizedek?

> **Pursue Wise Couns**
>
> The Bible gives no indication that L
> sought wise, godly counsel when
> he chose the beautiful land based
> primarily on appearances. As a res
> Lot—and his family—experienced
> much hardship and trouble.
> Godly people whom you can cons
> may include your pastor, a Christia
> financial planner, a Crown Money
> Map Coach, and a follower of Jesu
> who practices good stewardship a
> knows the joy of contentment.

② What characteristics did Lot exhibit in decision-making? What consequences resulted?

When we walk with God and seek His direction, how do our choices—and our underlying motivations—change?

③ What do you think God was emphasizing when He said to Abram, *"I am your shield, your very great reward"*? (See Genesis 15:1 NIV.)

In which area(s) of life do you need God to be your "shield"? Why?

How highly do people you know value their relationship with God? Do they value Him more highly than any other reward? Why or why not?

④ What things tend to hinder us from expressing our deepest longing to God, just as elderly Abram asked God for a child of his own?

Did You Know?

When you face key financial decisions, Crown Financial Ministries is ready to help. Request a confidential meeting with a Crown Money Map Coach in your area. Go to Crown.org/Coaches to chat live with an online coach or request a face-to-face meeting.

 # Reflect

Take just a few minutes now to quietly reflect on these inward-directed questions.

1. Which of Abram's characteristics would you like to demonstrate more often? Why?

2. Consider this Scripture passage: *"Be careful how you walk, not as unwise men but as wise, making the most of your time, because the days are evil"* (Ephesians 5:15-16 NASB). Like Lot, could you be making unwise choices that hinder your opportunities to serve the Lord? What might they be?

3. Why is it hard to seek God's "reward" rather than the alluring things of this world?

Who Was Melchizedek?

According to Hebrews 7:1-3, *"This Melchizedek was king of Salem and priest of God Most High. He met Abraham returning from the defeat of the kings and blessed him, and Abraham gave him a tenth of everything. First, his name means 'king of righteousness'; then also, 'king of Salem' means 'king of peace.' Without father or mother, without genealogy, without beginning of days or end of life, like the Son of God he remains a priest forever"* (NIV). He was a prophetic symbol of Jesus Christ. (See Psalm 110:4; Hebrews 5-7.)

 Cue DVD: Journey Notes - (2 minutes)

 # Journey Notes*

Chuck Bentley encourages you on your journey in this short "wrap up" presentation. Space is provided for you to jot down a few notes.

an alternative, you
use the monologue
ey Character's
pective" (found in
itional Teaching on
OVD).

God Is Our True Reward

God stated that He was Abram's reward and, amazingly, He can be our reward, too! Think about the following verses and how they apply to you: Psalm 16:11; 19:9-11; 37:4-6; 89:15-17; Proverbs 11:18; Isaiah 61:10; Matthew 16:24-27.

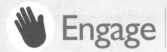
Personal Activity

Evaluate Your Priorities

Even if you don't realize it, every day we put our attention toward certain priorities over other less important things. Demands of work, life, money, family, and friends compete for our attention. Where are your priorities?

Consider these priorities in your life. What's most important to you?				
1 My Comfort	2	3	4	5 Serving People
1 Acquiring More	2	3	4	5 Living on Less
1 Keeping for myself	2	3	4	5 Generosity to Others

Abram showed us that he chose priorities that mattered to God, not man. He helped people, instead of being interested in gaining more wealth. He was content with less, instead of asking for more land and at the best location. Most importantly, he chose to give to God, rather than taking the spoils of battle for himself. We can learn much from Abram's walk with God and the chosen priorities of his life. (**Go to Crown.org/GodProvides to download the full "Evaluate Your Priorities" assessment.**)

Group Activity

Review the "Evaluate Your Priorities" scale above. Challenge the group to choose one thing to do together to begin serving others rather than seeking comfort, choosing less over more, or being generous rather than keeping for self. An example may be that each member will commit to preparing meals this week (instead of eating out) in order to put the money saved toward moving further to the right on the scale.

Have each person commit to this new priority between now and your next meeting. Appoint someone to e-mail the group during the week to encourage each other and share testimonies.

For Additional Exploration

Register online at Crown.org/GodProvides and follow the *Abram's Reward* links for more activities, **Next Step Resources**, and supporting materials such as **Evaluate Your Priorities Assessment** • **Biblical Background on Tithing** • **Additional Scriptures**

ABRAHAM AND ISAAC

"Mine or His?"

Adapted from Genesis 22:1-18

 Warm Up: *Participate in the short exercise given in the Facilitator's Guide.*

 Overview | *This section puts the film into context, setting the stage for discussion after you view the film.*

This session highlights the true story of Abraham and Isaac, his son. Often called "the Father of Faith," Abraham faced a difficult test when God commanded him to make an unusual and—based on human standards—seemingly nonsensical and cruel sacrifice. God used this test of obedience to see whether or not Abraham trusted Him fully and would, in faith, obediently make everything he had available for God's use.

Today we each have a choice. Will we listen to God's voice—through the Bible, prayer, and the wisdom of godly people? Will we not only seek God's will for our lives but obey Him faithfully—whether or not we know the final outcome? So much of our culture focuses on the "it's-all-about-me" mentality and demands to know final outcomes ahead of time.

Before facing this hard test, Abraham had already experienced a dynamic relationship with the living God, who told him to move his family to a new land. During all circumstances, God always fulfilled His previous promises to Abraham—including giving Abraham and his wife, Sarah, their beloved son, Isaac.

Like Abraham, we have opportunities to believe God—and that includes having faith that He will keep His promises and allowing Him to carry out His will for our lives. As we trust and obey Him, we will experience His peace and contentment regardless of our outward circumstances.

 Read *this film's foundational verses: Genesis 22:1-18.*

 Cue DVD: Feature Film - (20 minutes)

Discuss

These thought-provoking questions will help you discover the truths presented in this story. Study them on your own or discuss with others immediately after watching the film.

Did You Notice?

Before making the sacrifice, Abraham told his servant that he *and* Isaac would come back after worshiping God. How did Abraham know this? Check out God's promises in Genesis 15:1-6; 17:15-16, 21. Also see Hebrews 11:17-19.

1 Why do you think God told Abraham to sacrifice his son?

2 Do you think God tests followers of Jesus today? Why or why not?

3 In what way(s) has your faith in God faith been tested? What did you learn about yourself and God as a result?

4 How has God provided for the needs in your life? Describe a time God when provided in an unusual way.

Does God always provide what we need when we want it? Why or why not?

5 God challenged Abraham to trust Him with Isaac. When it comes to our possessions, and other gifts and blessings, why is it often difficult to recognize that they ultimately belong to God?

Why do some people have a hard time trusting God with their job situations, family problems, health issues, and other things?

Reflect

Take just a few minutes now to quietly reflect on these inward-directed questions.

1 In which particular area(s) might God be testing your willingness to obey Him fully and trust Him with your life and all that you have? How are you responding? What adjustments might you need to make?

2 Do you *really* believe that God will provide for your needs as He promises? How is this belief affecting the way you live? The lives of other people around you?

3 In the film, Abraham said that a sacrifice to God was an "act of worship." How might this relate to a sacrifice He may want you to make?

God's Sacrifice for Us

After stopping Abraham from sacrificing Isaac, God miraculously provided a ram to substitute in Isaac's place. This substitution points to the most amazing gift God could have given us. As recorded in the New Testament, Jesus Christ—God's only beloved Son, who was sinless—offered Himself in our place to provide for our deepest need—forgiveness of our sin (wrongdoing) (John 1:29; 1 John 4:10). Because of Jesus' sacrifice for all humankind, any person who confesses his/her sin and believes in faith that Jesus died for his/her sin will receive forgiveness and eternal life! (See 1 John 1:9; John 3:16.) God truly is *Jehovah Jireh*—the God who provides.

 Cue DVD: Journey Notes - (2 minutes)

Journey Notes*

Chuck Bentley encourages you on your journey in this short "wrap up" presentation. Space is provided for you to jot down a few notes.

an alternative, you
use the monologue
…ey Character's
…pective" (found in
…tional Teaching on
…DVD).

The Impact of Your Faith

Abraham is called the "Father of Faith" because his faith in God impacted not only his family but ultimately everyone who reads the Bible. How is your faith in God affecting the faith of other people?

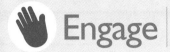

Engage

We are able to engage most fully with the new insights we discover when we apply them in very practical ways.

Personal Activity

What do you have in life? What do you truly value? What would you do if God asked you to give up something that He wanted to use for His purposes? Would you give it to Him freely? Would you put up a fight? Is He asking for something in your life right now?

Dedicate It to God

Make a list of the gifts you have in your life—family, career, money. When you are ready, hold a Dedication Service to God. Thank Him for supplying these gifts into your care and management. Acknowledge to Him that He is the giver and the owner of each gift. Dedicate each gift to God one-by-one and release each into His service.

People	Financial Accounts	Activities	Things

Go to Crown.org/GodProvides to download a full version of the "Dedicate It to God" worksheet.

Group Activity

Meet with your group to discuss the Dedication Service activity mentioned above. Challenge group members to individually follow through with this exercise on their own time. Pray together as a group asking God to show each person what God might be asking him or her to dedicate to Him.

In order to leave a lasting reminder with participants, symbolic items such as a small piece of rope (Isaac's bindings) or a bundle of small twigs tied together (wood from the altar) may be given to participants to represent the act of surrendering their will to the Lord. (Facilitators may want to distribute the "Dedicate It to God" worksheet to each person.)

For Additional Exploration

Register online at Crown.org/GodProvides and follow the *Abraham and Isaac* links for more activities, **Next Step Resources**, and supporting materials such as **Dedicate It to God Worksheet • Reflections on Romans 12:1-2**

RICH MAN ᴬᴺᴰ LAZARUS

"My Heart Choices Affect Eternity"

Adapted from Luke 16:19-31

Warm Up: *Participate in the short exercise given in the Facilitator's Guide.*

Overview

This section puts the film into context, setting the stage for discussion after you view the film.

Life after death is a hotly debated topic. "What happens after we die? How do our lives on earth affect how we spend eternity?"

This session is based on a parable Jesus told about a rich man and Lazarus, a beggar—and the afterlife. As the film portrays, there is an eternal heaven (Paradise) and a separate and eternal hell—a place of torment. The Bible emphasizes this. However, it also teaches that what we believe and place our faith in during our earthly lives determines our eternal destiny. If we place our faith in money and possessions, for example, we will be left with nothing and spend eternity in hell separated from God. But if we place our faith in Jesus Christ, we will spend eternity in His presence. That is a step of "saving" faith—leading to salvation; no one can earn eternity in heaven by good deeds. (See Ephesians 2:8-9.)

The other key theme of this session deals with riches and poverty. Poor people have coexisted with rich people since humankind's earliest days. It is not wrong to be rich or poor. However, in the Bible—God's Word for us today—God says that earthly wealth is temporary and provided to us in order to meet our needs and the needs of others. He commands His followers to lovingly, compassionately, and generously use their resources to help people in need.

 Read *this film's foundational verses:* Luke 16:19-31

 Cue DVD: Feature Film - (15 minutes)

Discuss

These thought-provoking questions will help you discover the truths presented in the story. Study them on your own or discuss with others immediately after watching the film.

1 What did you think about and feel as you watched the film? Why?

2 How might a person's use of money and other resources reflect his/her perspective on the afterlife?

> ### Think About It
> If someone were to review your calendar and use of money over the past six months, what would they discover about your priorities? View of possessions? Commitment to reach out to people in need?

3 In what ways does society favor wealthy people and discriminate against poor people? Why does this happen? Why don't more people help the poor?

4 In Jesus' parable, Abraham told the formerly rich man that if his brothers would not listen to Moses and the prophets they would not listen to someone raised from the dead. Do you agree? Why or why not?

5 What attitudes and beliefs can hinder us from helping people in need?

How can we know when we are giving enough—of our time, money, other resources—to needy people?

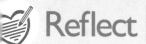

Reflect

Take just a few minutes now to quietly reflect on these inward-directed questions.

1 What is your "take-away" truth from this session?

2 Just as Lazarus lay at the rich man's gate, people in need may be near your "gate." How will you help one or more of them—in small or large ways?

3 In the same way that the rich man influenced his five brothers, you are influencing other people through your beliefs and use of resources. What kind of example are you setting for your friends, family, and coworkers?

> ### The Reality of Heaven and Hell
>
> Many people do not believe in hell or that placing personal faith in Jesus Christ is the only way to heaven, but the Bible speaks to these issues.
>
> **Jesus: the only way to God and heaven**
> John 3:16; 10:9; 14:6; Acts 4:10-12; Romans 5:9; 6:23; Ephesians 2:8-9.
>
> **Heaven:**
> Matthew 6:19-20; 25:31; Luke 15:7; John 14:2; Philippians 3:20-21; 1 Thessalonians 4:16-17; 1 Peter 1:4; Revelation 22:5.
>
> **Hell:**
> Isaiah 33:14; Matthew 3:12; 5:22-30; 8:12; 10:28; 13:42; 18:8-9; James 3:6; 2 Peter 2:4; Revelation 14:10; 20:10.

Cue DVD: Journey Notes - (2 minutes)

Journey Notes*

Chuck Bentley encourages you on your journey in this short "wrap up" presentation. Space is provided for you to jot down a few notes.

an alternative, you use the monologue ey Character's pective" (found in tional Teaching on DVD).

> ### Heaven Is for Everyone
>
> The Bible says that anyone—rich or poor, sick or well, unknown or famous—can receive eternal life in heaven simply by placing personal faith in Jesus Christ.
>
> Be sure to view the film *Lifted Up*, included in this series, for more information on this vital subject.

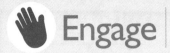

Engage

We are able to engage most fully with the new insights we discover when we apply them in very practical ways.

Personal Activity

Sadly, the rich man did not leave the legacy he intended. How are you doing at building the financial and spiritual legacy you desire? Complete the "Legacy Building" assessment.

	How Are You Influencing People Spiritually?	What Do Your Finances Say About Your Lifestyle?	How Would You Rate Your Generosity?	Do You Have An Up-to-Date Estate Plan and Will?
Current Evaluation				
What Needs to Be Changed?				
When Will These Changes Occur?				

You may download the full "Legacy Building" assessment by following the *Rich Man and Lazarus* links at Crown.org/GodProvides.

Group Activity

In the beginning session of this learning experience, your group was asked to identify someone in need of help. Who will you help with a service project or practical need? What resources, skills, and talents does your group collectively have to help meet that need? Now is the time to action your ideas and enjoy the blessings of serving others. Make contact with the person you will help and set a date to make it happen. Assign tasks to each one in the group, ensuring everyone participates and is engaged. Ask God to bless your efforts and the lives of those involved.

For Additional Exploration

Register online at Crown.org/GodProvides and follow the *Rich Man and Lazarus* links for more activities, **Next Step Resources**, and supporting materials such as **Legacy Building Assessment • Additional Scriptures to Study • Family Projects**

LIFTED UP

"My Hope for the Future"
Adapted from Numbers 21:4-9 and John 3:1-17

 Warm Up: *Participate in the short exercise given in the Facilitator's Guide.*

Overview | *This section puts the film into context, setting the stage for discussion after you view the film.*

After God miraculously delivered the ancient Israelites from slavery in Egypt, they rebelled against Him and spent forty years wandering in the wilderness. Then, as the remaining Israelites neared the land God chose for them, they spoke against Him again—and against Moses, their leader.

As the film for this session portrays, God sent poisonous snakes to bite these rebellious people. Confessing that they were wrong, the people asked Moses to pray for God to remove the snakes. Following God's directions, Moses put a bronze snake on a pole, and anybody dying of snakebite who looked at the pole lived. God mercifully provided a way for those people to escape the consequences of their sin (wrongdoing).

Many years later, Jesus—the Son of God—came to earth to save us from our sins and give us spiritual life—salvation. One night, a religious leader named Nicodemus visited Jesus. Their conversation reveals that any person can be spiritually transformed and enjoy a personal relationship with the living God of the universe.

The Israelites looked at the bronze snake lifted up on a pole, believing in God's remedy for their condition. In the same way, people today can believe in Jesus, who was lifted up on a cross to bear the sins of humankind, died, and rose from the dead. Through Jesus' loving sacrifice, each of us can receive forgiveness for sin, a spiritual rebirth, a new life being transformed by God, and the certainty of eternal life in heaven.

 Read this film's foundational verses: John 3:1-17.

 Cue DVD: Feature Film - (19 minutes)

Discuss

These thought-provoking questions will help you discover the truths presented in the story. Study them on your own or discuss with others immediately after watching the film.

1 God sent snakes among the ancient Israelites when they rebelled against God. What are some ways people rebel against God today?

What are some of the consequences you've seen as a result?

2 The people were healed when they confessed their sins and turned back to God. Have you ever confessed your sins to God? What issues keep people from doing that today?

Verses to Ponder

• *"For God so loved the world that he gave his one and only Son, that whoever believes in him shall not perish but have eternal life. For God did not send his Son into the world to condemn the world, but to save the world through him"* (John 3:16-17 NIV).

• *"If we confess our sins, He [Jesus] is faithful and righteous to forgive us our sins and to cleanse us from all unrighteousness [wrongdoing]"* (1 John 1:9 NASB).

3 What did Nicodemus struggle to understand about Jesus and His teachings?

In what way(s) did you identify with Nicodemus? Why?

4 Jesus said that God loved and wanted to save the world, not condemn it. How did His being "lifted up" make this possible?

Reflect

Take just a few minutes now to quietly reflect on these inward-directed questions.

If you are not following Jesus...

Do you find it easy or hard to understand and receive God's love, which He demonstrated by sending Jesus to be lifted up on a cross for your sin? Why?

Is there anything keeping you from responding to His invitation to be "born again"?

If you follow Jesus...

Think about your current walk with Jesus. What things might there be which keep you from going deeper with Him?

How committed are you to knowing Jesus better—through fellowship with other followers of Jesus, Bible study, prayer, obedience?

> ### "Born Again"
> ### (John 3:3)
>
> To be "born again" is to start a personal relationship with God by believing in Jesus—who committed no sin (wrongdoing) (2 Corinthians 5:21) yet died on the cross (1 Peter 2:24) as a sacrifice for our sin. People who believe in Jesus and invite Him into their lives as their Lord and Savior are "born of the Spirit"—the Spirit of God who renews human hearts and lives within every follower of Jesus. (See 2 Corinthians 5:17; Titus 3:5.)

 Cue DVD: Journey Notes - (2 minutes)

Journey Notes*

Chuck Bentley encourages you on your journey in this short "wrap up" presentation. Space is provided for you to jot down a few notes.

an alternative, you
use the monologue
ey Character's
spective" (found in
tional Teaching on
VD).

> ### "Just Look"
>
> Just as little Benjamin encouraged his mother to "just look" at the bronze snake and live, Nicodemus had to set aside his pride and "just look" at Jesus—who was "lifted up" for all people. This decision to believe is one every person must make.

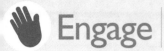

Engage

We are able to engage most fully with the new insights we discover when we apply them in very practical ways.

Activities

If you would like to learn more about Jesus, the Bible, or Christianity in general . . .

Pursue answers, just like Nicodemus did! For example, read the book of John in the Bible and pay close attention to what Jesus said and did—and why He came to earth. Discuss your questions and issues with a follower of Jesus. And if you need additional guidance or instruction, ask for it. More information can be found by following the *Lifted Up* links at Crown.org/GodProvides.

If you are ready now to become a follower of Jesus Christ—to be "born again"—please turn to page 31 in this guide.

If you follow Jesus...

On a sheet of paper, briefly summarize your core, faith-related beliefs (concerning the Bible, Jesus, heaven, God's forgiveness, and so forth). Then compare these beliefs to how your beliefs influence your daily life. If sin has entered your life, remember what the ancient Israelites learned—confess your sin to God and receive His forgiveness and healing. Perhaps the following questions will be helpful:

- **How passionate am I about following Jesus?**

- **Which things (positive and/or negative) are affecting my relationship with Jesus?**

- **What changes might I need to make to strengthen my relationship with Jesus? To reflect my heart's desire and the unique plan I feel God has for my life?**

If your friends and/or family members do not follow Jesus, think about how He related to Nicodemus. In what way(s) might you share the love and truth of Jesus with them?

For Additional Exploration

Register online at Crown.org/GodProvides and follow the *Lifted Up* links for **Next Step Resources** and additional study and activities, including Web links and Bible verses about becoming a follower of Jesus.

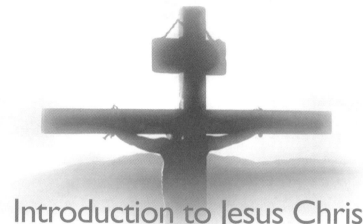

Introduction to Jesus Christ

Did you know that the God of the universe highly values relationships? This was true at the beginning of time when He created man and woman and walked in fellowship with them. And it's still true today. God wants to begin a relationship with you. In fact, He has a single, clear plan for anyone who wants to begin a relationship with God through Jesus Christ.

1. God loves you deeply.

God loves you and He wants to spend eternity with you.

"For God so loved the world, that He gave His only begotten Son, that whoever believes in Him shall not perish, but have eternal life" (John 3:16 NASB).

2. Unfortunately, we are separated from God.

Because God is holy and perfect, no sin can abide in His presence. Everyone has sinned (done wrong), and the consequence of sin is separation from God.

"All have sinned and fall short of the glory of God" (Romans 3:23 NASB).

"Your iniquities [sins] have made a separation between you and your God" (Isaiah 59:2 NASB).

3. God's only provision to bridge this gap is Jesus Christ.

Many religions claim there are numerous ways to know God. But the Bible is clear that Jesus is God's only way to eternal life with Him.

"I am the way, and the truth, and the life; no one comes to the Father but through Me" (Jesus speaking – John 14:6 NASB).

"God demonstrates His own love toward us, in that while we were yet sinners, Christ died for us" (Romans 5:8 NASB).

4. This relationship is a gift from God.

Our efforts to reach God can never achieve the perfection God requires. The only solution was for God to provide it to us as a gift. God sent Jesus to bear our sins on the cross, paying our sin penalty forever. He exchanged His righteousness for our sin and guilt. By faith, we receive the gift we could never deserve.

"For by grace you have been saved through faith; and that not of yourselves, it is the gift of God; not as a result of works, so that no one may boast" (Ephesians 2:8-9 NASB).

5. We must each receive Jesus Christ individually.

Each of us will be judged for our own sin.

"It is appointed for men to die once and after this comes judgment" (Hebrews 9:27 NASB).

We can continue to bear the responsibility of our sin and pay the consequences on our own, or we can receive the gift of Jesus' righteousness, be completely forgiven, and hear God declare us "Not Guilty!"

If you desire to begin a relationship with Jesus Christ, we encourage you to begin right now. Talk to God by praying a prayer similar to this one:

"God I need You. I invite Jesus to come into my life as my Savior and Lord and to make me the person You want me to be. Thank You for forgiving my sins and for giving me the gift of eternal life."

You can learn more about becoming a follower of Jesus at Crown.org/GodProvides.

Family Guide

While the *God Provides™ Learning Experience* is recommended for all ages, we recognize that adjustments may be necessary to accommodate younger participants in a family setting. This guide offers some helpful suggestions to facilitate learning in each of the sessions.

> *These biblical stories portray God's Word with emotional intensity. Parents, please preview each film to evaluate your young children's readiness to watch.*

Please keep these points in mind:

Warm Up	A simple warm-up activity is always helpful to create interest.
Overview	You may need to put the story into a more concrete context.
Discuss	Try to reword the questions in simpler terms, but keep the main idea. (A couple of examples are provided to get you started.)
Reflect	Instead of quiet reflection, you may want to look up and read a related verse in the Bible or read the information in one of the lesson's shaded boxes.
Journey Notes	Ask the children if they have any questions about what was said or emphasize a key point that was mentioned.
Engage	The activities should be scaled to levels appropriate to the children's ages.

Be sure to register online at Crown.org/GodProvides for additional information.

Warm Up

Ask the children to give *synonyms* (words or phrases that mean the same thing) for these words (call them out one at a time, giving time for responses): poor; jar; neighbor; money. (Feel free to think of other words related to the story.)

Overview

Sometimes people get into situations where they need to pay for something, but they don't have enough money. The family in this story was in that kind of situation. The people that wanted payment were upset and acted unkindly. But God knew what the family needed. He provided in a very special way, using something they already had.

Discuss

1. What do you think the boys were feeling when the unkind men visited them?

2. Did the boys help their mother follow Elisha's instructions? What did they do?

3. How did the boys and their mother feel after she paid the men?

Reflect

Read aloud the information titled "God Can Use the Most Basic Things" in the box on page 10.

Engage

"What do we have?" Make a list of family resources you have that could be used to help another person in need (money, skills, items of value). Allow the children to offer their own ideas and possessions as the family brainstorms together.

"Who can we help?" Identify an individual or family who needs help or assistance. Record your ideas and begin praying about this future service project.

JEREMIAH'S CALL
FAMILY GUIDE

Warm Up

Pretend for a minute that we had to move to a different country—a place where they speak a different language. What changes might we see from our lives now? (language, money, homes, food, etc.)

Overview

Many years ago God's people were forced to move to a different country. They were very sad, and missed their homes and their former way of life. Many wondered why God had allowed this to happen to them. But God had not forgotten them! He sent a letter through His prophet, Jeremiah, to encourage them and to give them hope.

Discuss

1. Why were the Israelites sad about their living situation? What did they want instead?

2. What God said to the Israelites through Jeremiah was very different from what the false prophets had been saying. How can we know what God really says?

3. When we have a problem, what is the first and best thing we can do to find an answer to the problem?

4. Sometimes bad things can happen, even to good people. Does this mean that God does not love them?

Reflect

Read aloud Jeremiah 29:11. Talk about God's loving plans that He has for each of us.

Engage

Plan a family Prayer Walk. Depending on the children's ages, you might want to limit it to your neighborhood. Pause periodically and pray for the neighbors in that area.

ABRAM'S REWARD

Warm Up

Do you know what a reward is? (Allow time for answers, and maybe give an example.)
What is the best reward you can think of?

Overview

Abram loved his nephew Lot. He took Lot with him on his journey, and even let him
choose the best land for his animals. When Lot and his family were captured, Abram
and his men rescued them. Because Abram loved the Lord, he gave a large gift to
Melchizedek, the priest of God.

Discuss

1. Lot chose the best lands for his herds. What should he have done instead?

2. How did Lot's choice lead to trouble?

3. What was Abram's true reward?

4. God granted Abram his greatest desire, a son named Isaac. What is your
   greatest desire? Have you talked to God about it?

Reflect

Read Genesis 14:22-23. Abram wouldn't take anything from the wicked king of Sodom.
He wanted people to know that it was God who had blessed him. How has God blessed
our family?

Engage

Review the *"Evaluate Your Priorities"* scale on page 18. Challenge the family to do something this week to begin serving others rather than seeking comfort, choosing less over
more, or being generous rather than keeping for self. An example may be that you could
give up eating out this week in order to use the money saved to meet a family goal.

After the exercise is completed, get the family members back together to talk about the
experience. You'll discover that few of us ever regret sacrifices made to show love and
kindness to others.

ABRAHAM AND ISAAC

FAMILY GUIDE

Warm Up

[Note: the scene leading up to the offering of Isaac may be intense for younger viewers.] When your mom or dad asks you to do something, do you sometimes say, "But why?" Sometimes a parent will answer back, "Because I said so." Well, what if God asked you to do something, would you do it? (pause for responses).

Overview

Abraham loved God and always tried to obey Him. When Abraham was very old, God gave him and his wife, Sarah, a son, whom they named Isaac. And God promised Abraham that the whole world would be blessed through Isaac and Isaac's children. One day God asked Abraham to do a very hard thing—to give Isaac back to Him, meaning that Isaac would have to die. Although Abraham didn't completely understand why, he obeyed God. He knew that God could be trusted to keep His promise. And God did! At the last minute, He provided an animal for Abraham to offer to God instead of Isaac.

Discuss

1. Why did people make sacrifices to God?

2. How do people worship God today?

3. What are things that we can offer to God as worship?

Reflect

Read the "God's Sacrifice for Us" box on page 21. Talk about how Jesus took our place by offering Himself for our sins, taking the punishment for the things we did wrong.

Engage

Adapt the Group Activity on page 22 for your family. Make sure each family member participates and completes the downloadable "Dedicate It to God" worksheet.

RICH MAN AND LAZARUS

FAMILY GUIDE

Warm Up

[Note: this film graphically depicts Lazarus' ill condition and the rich man's torment in hell. You should preview the film and use discretion with younger viewers.] Do you know what a parable is? A parable is an interesting story that is told to illustrate a particular lesson.

Overview

Jesus told the story of a rich man and a poor man. The rich man had many things, but did not show kindness or share with the poor man, Lazarus. Eventually, both men die. Lazarus goes to heaven (Paradise) and the rich man is punished in hell (not for being rich but for being selfish).

Discuss

1. Why didn't the rich man help Lazarus? What do you think God wanted him to do?

2. Where did the rich man go after he died? Where did Lazarus go? Why?

3. What does God want us to do with the things we have?

Reflect

How would it feel if you were very hungry, but no one would give you even a little bit to eat? How should we react when we see a person in need?

Engage

Adapt the Group Activity on page 26 for your family.

If you haven't yet identified someone to help, ask God to show your family someone like Lazarus whom you can serve. It may be someone in your neighborhood, at school, or even at church. God may want you to give that person something or to do something for him or her. God will bless you for giving (Acts 20:35).

LIFTED UP
FAMILY GUIDE

Warm Up

[Note: the scene of the snakebite and the scenes of Jesus on the cross may be intense for younger viewers.] When you've done something wrong, how do you feel? (pause for answers) Everyone does things that are wrong. That's a problem, because God never does anything wrong. Because He loves us so much, God has made a way for us to be forgiven and to live with Him forever.

Overview

When people do bad things, like God's children did in the desert long ago, punishment is the result. When the people were hurt by the snakes, they realized that God was angry at their sin, and they were very sorry. Because God loved them, He told Moses to make an image of a snake and put it up on a pole. When the hurt people looked at it, they were well again!

Many years later, God sent His Son, Jesus, as the way for all people to be saved from the punishment they deserved. People today need to confess their sin to God and trust Jesus—the one who was punished instead of them—as their Savior.

Discuss

1. What was the little boy trying to get his mother to do?

2. What happened when she looked at the bronze snake?

3. Just like the bronze snake, Jesus was lifted up. Why did Jesus let this happen to Himself?

4. What good things can happen to us because of what Jesus did?

Reflect

Read the "Verses to Ponder" on page 28. Ask what it means to "confess" (to tell someone what you did wrong). Talk about why this is important.

Engage

Distribute to each child a sheet of paper divided into 4 quadrants. Ask the children to draw 4 things: a cross, an empty tomb (cave), a sad face, and a happy face. Then discuss the importance of these concepts: the sacrifice of Jesus on the cross, His triumph over death, confession of our sins, and new life in Christ.

FACILITATOR'S GUIDE

Suggested Flow for Each Session

- **Open / Warm Up (3–4 minutes)**
- **Read the Overview (1–2 minutes)**
- **Read the Foundational Scripture Verses (1–2 minutes)**
- **Play Feature Film (12–20 minutes)**
- **Discuss (15–20 minutes)**
- **Reflect (5 minutes)**
- **Engage (3 minutes)**
- **Play Journey Notes (2–3 minutes)**
- **Wrap Up / Close (5–7 minutes)**

Important Reminder

You are facilitating a discovery process. Remember that God is the true teacher. As the Holy Spirit applies valuable lessons from His Word, everyone benefits and grows. This guide gives tips and techniques to help you facilitate a group with highest impact.

Be sure to register online at Crown.org/ GodProvides for more suggestions and information.

Tips for Facilitating the Learning Experience

 Open / Warm Up / Overview (5–8 minutes)

To leave time for meaningful discussion after the film, keep your opening comments brief. Welcome participants, thank them for coming, and remind them to turn off cell phones. Open with prayer. Guide participants into the "warm-up" exercise. (For additional warm-up ideas, please go to Crown.org/GodProvides) After the exercise, read the Overview and the foundational Scripture verses. You will then view the feature film.

 Discuss (15–20 minutes)

You may choose to follow the questions listed in this Companion Guide or simply refer to them from the screen (they are also included on the DVD). Please go to Crown.org/GodProvides for detailed tips for group discussion and relating one-to-one.

 Reflect (5 minutes)

Your time will vary in this segment depending on each film's length. Individuals quietly review aspects of the lesson and contemplate potential application to their lives and specific situations.

 Engage (3 minutes)

Research shows that true life-change occurs when people actively participate in new lessons just learned. Review the individual application exercises and encourage participants to commit to taking these next steps. Assign a leader to oversee any group activities.

 Journey Notes (2–3 minutes)

In each video segment (2–3 minutes), Chuck Bentley encourages participants and recaps lessons learned. Encourage participants to take notes in the space provided. As an alternative, you may use the monologue "A Key Character's Perspective" (found in Additional Teaching on the DVD).

 Wrap Up / Close (5–7 minutes)

Follow the Journey Notes segment with any brief, supportive statements you feel led to share. Choose a verse to share or have someone read it to close your group time. (Suggested closing Scripture verses are provided at Crown.org/GodProvides.) Lead the group in a brief prayer asking God to give wisdom and discernment for next steps.

In order to enhance the film viewing experience, make sure you have proper lighting, a good sound system and a high-quality DVD player.

WIDOW AND OIL
FACILITATOR'S GUIDE

Relating to Your Group's Needs

Because *Widow and Oil* is the shortest of the *God Provides*™ films (12 minutes, including credits), your group discussion may need to be extended. If so, we recommend referring to the "Crying Out to God" box on page 8 and reviewing the referenced Scriptures. (There are additional discussion questions at Crown.org/GodProvides.)

Groups may often have participants with pressing needs who will relate directly to the widow. However, you also may have those in your group who are in a position to help meet the needs of others. Both can discover valuable truths to apply from this session.

Warm-Up Exercise

I'm going to hold up some cards on which I have written various types of people. I'd like you to respond out loud with some needs that each may encounter. (Examples might include: **elderly person** – needing the company of others, **single mom** – needing someone to help watch her children, **newlywed couple** – needing financial coaching, **disabled person** – needing a ride to town, and **widow** – needing help with yard work.)

Often we can help each another meet specific needs. God, who loves us and is aware of our situations, is the greatest provider of all our needs! And when we ask Him for help, He may use what we already have to meet those needs—a godly friend who handles finances well, a church group that mobilizes to clean up a flooded basement, or an unrecognized skill or talent we can use to earn more income.

Highlighted Resource for Additional Exploration

It is important to familiarize yourself with this resource, which is referenced in the Engage activities.

What Do You Have? Inventory – *Useful worksheet for listing assets, skills, and other resources that can be utilized to better one's financial situation.*

More Helpful Resources and Links *(Crown.org/GodProvides)*

- **Financial Stewardship Assessment**
- **Crown Money Map Coaches**
- **Benevolence Ministry Resource**
- **Topical Videos**
- **Next Step Resources**

Relating to Your Group's Needs

This lesson may cause participants to want to share difficult situations in which they are involved or currently experiencing. As you facilitate, look for opportunities to gently reinforce the main points of this film:

- God tells us to return to the basics: 1) earn income using what you have, 2) care for your home and family, 3) contribute to your community (Jeremiah 29:5-7). Getting good rest, eating well, and doing something for someone else are simple habits that benefit anyone in a stressful situation.

- God has unique plans for each person (Jeremiah 29:11).

- He calls us to seek Him with all our heart and to wait (Jeremiah 29:12-13).

- We can pray for people in authority over us—even if we don't agree with our current situation (Romans 13).

The Prayer Walk is an excellent group activity you'll want to consider. As they become involved, participants will have opportunity to pray for local, state, and national leaders. See the group activity for more details.

Warm-Up Exercise

Do you know people who have made the most out of a difficult situation? Describe to the group how they overcame adversity, what impressed you most, and how they had a positive influence on others. (Examples: Joni Eareckson Tada, Elisabeth Elliot, George Washington Carver, Job.)

In this film, we'll see that—even in the middle of their trials—God provides the exiled Israelites with specific guidance and hope.

Highlighted Resource for Additional Exploration

It is important to familiarize yourself with this resource.

Debt Reduction Plan – *In our culture, difficult situations are often caused by excessive debt. The Debt Reduction Plan allows people to organize their debts and systematically begin a payoff process.*

More Helpful Resources and Links *(Crown.org/GodProvides)*

- **Job Satisfaction Survey**
- ***Personality I.D.® Profile***
- **Next Step Resources**

ABRAM'S REWARD
FACILITATOR'S GUIDE

Relating to Your Group's Needs

In *Abram's Reward*, participants will observe how Abram and Lot made several key decisions dealing with people and possessions. As you facilitate this week's session, look for opportunities to show group members the importance of:

- Being satisfied with less rather than accumulating more.
- Putting people and relationships ahead of gaining material possessions.
- Being generous toward others rather than hoarding for one's self.

Warm-Up Exercise

When I say the word *reward*, what comes to mind? (pause for response) What is the best reward that you can think of? (pause for response)

There are many rewards in this life, aren't there? During today's session, we're going to consider the lives of two men, Abram (later renamed Abraham), and his nephew, Lot. They made quite different choices, and one man received the best reward anyone could dream of—one we, too, can receive.

Highlighted Resource for Additional Exploration

Evaluate Your Priorities Assessment *– A simple worksheet to help you evaluate and record your life's priorities as it relates to generosity, serving others, and material possessions*

More Helpful Resources and Links *(Crown.org/GodProvides)*

- **A Biblical Background on Tithing**
- **"Giving and Tithing" topical resource**
- **Next Step Resources**

ABRAHAM AND ISAAC
FACILITATOR'S GUIDE

Relating to Your Group's Needs

At more than 19 minutes long, *Abraham and Isaac* is the longest of the *God Provides*™ films. You will need to manage your time well in order to give proper time to this week's important discussion.

A helpful resource at Crown.org/GodProvides, "Abraham, a Long History of Obeying God," will give you additional background information on Abraham's life and his walk with God. God changed Abram's name to Abraham meaning "father of many nations" (Genesis 17:5).

It may be difficult for some participants to relate Abraham's offering of Isaac to modern-day examples of sacrificing to God. Come prepared with several examples of sacrifices people make to honor the Lord. (For example, forgoing additional income for mom to stay at home; making do with an older car to give to others in need; serving God far from home or family, etc.)

Warm-Up Exercise

Before we view today's film, let's do a brief exercise. Does everyone have a pencil or pen? Let's all stand. Take your pen or pencil in hand and hold it tightly in front of you. Think about this: When it comes to your money and possessions, how tightly are you holding on to them? If God wanted to use those things you loved most, how would you respond?

Now loosen your grip, holding your pencil or pen gently in your hand—palm up. If we hold our possessions loosely, in an open palm, and always make them available to God, He can freely use them for His purposes. This session's film highlights a difficult choice Abraham had to make concerning his son, Isaac.

Highlighted Resource for Additional Exploration

This form is used with this session's Engage activities.

> **"Dedicate It to God" Worksheet** *– A helpful form used to facilitate a dedication service to God*

> **More Helpful Resources and Links** *(Crown.org/GodProvides)*
>
> - **Abraham, a Long History of Obeying God**
> - **Romans 12:1-2 (verses for further study)**
> - **Next Step Resources**

RICH MAN AND LAZARUS
FACILITATOR'S GUIDE

Relating to Your Group's Needs

The topics of heaven, hell, and the use of a person's material possessions may be new to some participants. Most likely there will be differing opinions on this subject, which can lead to lively discussion. It will be important for you as the facilitator to keep the group "on topic" and away from tangents.

The following statements and Scriptures may help bring discussion back on point.

- Money is often an outside indicator of what is going on spiritually inside a person's heart (Matthew 6:21).

- It is not a sin to be wealthy, nor is it necessarily a virtue to be poor. God is ultimately the one who gives a person wealth (Deuteronomy 8:17-18).

- Being lukewarm and relying on wealth instead of God is displeasing to God (Revelation 3:16-17).

Warm-Up Exercise

If you could, would you choose to know the time of your death? (pause for response) If you did know, what changes might you make? Why? (pause for response)

During this session, we will look at issues related to heaven and hell and also explore the importance of using our resources to help people in need.

Highlighted Resource for Additional Exploration

This tool is referenced in the Engage personal activity.

Legacy Building Assessment – *A tool designed to help people evaluate long-term financial and spiritual practices that will build a God-honoring legacy.*

More Helpful Resources and Links *(Crown.org/GodProvides)*

- **Next Step Resources**
- **Additional Scriptures**
- **Additional Service Project Ideas**

LIFTED UP
FACILITATOR'S GUIDE

Relating to Your Group's Needs

Lifted Up is more than 18 minutes in length. You will need to manage your time well in order to give proper time to this week's important discussion.

Most small groups are comprised of two types of people: those who are followers of Jesus and those who are not. In today's session, it's important for believers and seekers alike to make personal application. Helpful questions in the **Reflect** and **Engage** portions of this session are designed with each category of participant in mind.

Chuck Bentley invites people to become followers of Jesus in the closing video segment. Also, he challenges those who already follow Jesus to rededicate their lives to Him.

See the *"Introduction to Jesus Christ"* on pages 31 and 32 for additional helpful information and a sample prayer.

Warm-Up Exercise

Have you ever looked at your birth certificate? (pause for response) What are some of the main items listed on the certificate? (again, pause for response)

A birth certificate usually describes the unique date and time we each entered into this world. (For example, December 28, 1970 at 10:01 a.m.) Did you know that Jesus told of a *second* birth in the Bible in John Chapter 3? Today's film, *Lifted Up*, powerfully portrays Jesus' encounter with a man who was seeking the truth.

More Helpful Resources and Links
(Crown.org/GodProvides)

- **Next Step Resources**
- **Bible verses about becoming a follower of Jesus**
- **Links to inspirational videos and resources**

SHARING THE *GOD PROVIDES*™ MESSAGE
'the little we have can make a difference'

Poor people in rural Africa were astonished.

They literally felt they had nothing ... then they learned that even the land they lived on could become productive in God's economy. "From what we have learned from the films ... we will be able to make better use of our land and from that, we will have more than enough."

Imagine impoverished people learning that their little becomes more than enough when God provides!

The Vision

You've experienced the *God Provides*™ films for yourself.

You know that Crown Financial Ministries® has been the comprehensive source for the best in resources for biblical financial stewardship for more than 30 years.

And you can surely see how engaging hearts through storytelling will reach visual learners in nations around the world — both those who read and those who can't.

We believe God wants us to use these films to present biblical truths in a powerful way, so viewers can experience a fresh connection with God and find hope in Him no matter their circumstances.

Your Part

You can personally join in sharing this message.

We need your help to translate all six of these short films, and the accompanying learning tools, into 25 major languages. In Africa alone, we have an opportunity to provide these films to 20,000 government high schools that would make this a part of their curriculum!

We are engaging with at least 50 faith-based mission organizations worldwide to distribute the films. You'll be touching lives in Africa, Asia-Pacific, Europe, India, North America, and Latin America ... regions populated by nearly 70% of the world's people.

They're just waiting to hear that God cares ... and that He will provide.

And He can provide ... through you. Just give today to help us translate and prepare the materials! The cost to translate each film is $15,000. Perhaps you can provide a portion of this cost—gifts of $100, $50, or even $25 will be combined to make the translations happen, so whatever you purpose to give, God can use! Simply donate online or by calling us toll-free today.

Crown.org/DonateOnline
1-800-249-6320

CROWN FINANCIAL
MINISTRIES

Crown.org/GodProvides
Your *Online* Companion

✔ Connect with Others

Join *God Provides*™ Facebook group and read about people's experiences on the *God Provides*™ blog.

✔ Additional Exploration

God Provides™ is just a step in your journey. Learn more about free practical tools that can help you.

✔ Facilitator Tools

Are you facilitating *God Provides*™ in your family or church? Obtain free additional information and tips to enhance your experience.

/ Next Steps

Purchase the *God Provides*™ *Learning Experience* resources direct from Crown, or find a Christian retailer in your local area that offers them.

/ Ideas for Large Group Screening

Want to show *God Provides*™ to groups larger than 100 people? Purchase a large group viewing license.

Register online at Crown.org/GodProvides or call 1-800-249-6320.

Next Step Resources

Need help taking the next practical step after the *God Provides™ Learning Experience?*

MONEYLIFE™
BASICS SERIES

Each topic in this pocket-sized series offers biblical wisdom, practical advice, and positive encouragement. Get immediate, first-aid response to everyday financial questions.

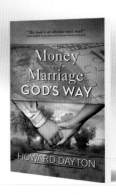

Money and Marriage
GOD'S WAY

More than a practical book on money, this resource discusses the root causes of financial strife in marriages today and offers solutions to avoid or repair issues that can affect the health of your marriage.

YOUR MONEY MAP

Learn the 7 proven practical steps to true financial freedom in this six-part video guide hosted by Crown Cofounder Howard Dayton. Consider this resource your personal financial coaching session!